PUTT! PUTT! POP!

Glenview, Illinois • Boston, Massachusetts • Chandler, Arizona
Shoreview, Minnesota • Upper Saddle River, New Jersey

Putt! Putt! Putt!

Izzy did not go fast.

2 He did not zip up the hill.

Putt! Putt! Putt!

Izzy had a dent.

Izzy had a lot of rust.

Putt! Putt! Pop!

Pop? Izzy had to stop!

Where can he get help?

4

Where can Izzy go?

Ted had to get him.

"Come with me," said Ted.

5

Ted had to buzz!

Ted had to zap!

Buzz! Zap! Buzz! Zap!

6

"Come and look," said Ted.

Ted had a big job.

But Ted did it.

7

Izzy can vroom!

Izzy is glad!